W O   ·   U E S

FA   DE?

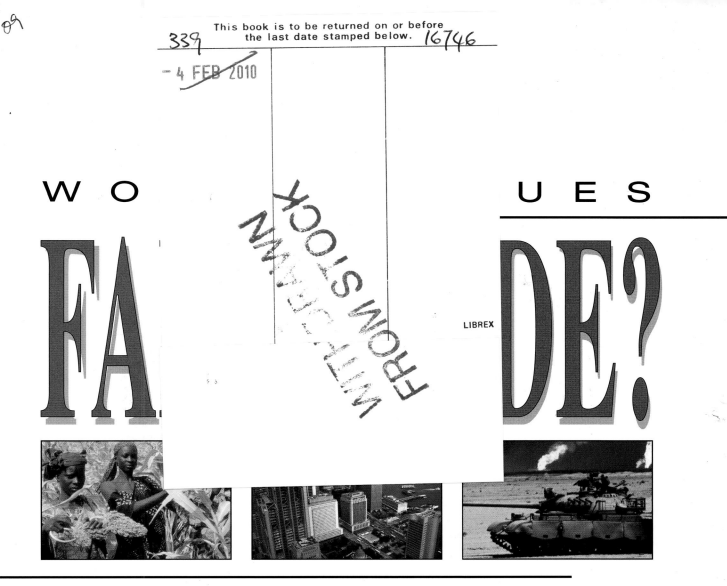

LIBREX

A look at the way the world is today

Adrian Cooper

D0336260

Fair trade

ABOUT THIS BOOK

FAIR TRADE? looks at all aspects of this important and varied subject. This book will help you to understand trade and the issues behind it.

You will learn more about the effects of trade on our global community and see how trade affects every one of us, each day of our lives.

You will find information on many aspects of trade – what is fair trade, why isn't trade always fair and what can be done about it. You will also find out about organisations that have been set up to promote FAIRTRADE products.

New edition printed in 2006
© Aladdin Books Ltd 2005
Produced by Aladdin Books Ltd
2/3 Fitzroy Mews, London W1T 6DF

ISBN 978–07496–5521–1 (Hardback)
ISBN 978–07496–7012–2 (Paperback)

First published in 2005 by

Franklin Watts	Franklin Watts Australia
338 Euston Road	Hachette Children's Books
London	Level 17/207 Kent Street
NW1 3BH	Sydney NSW 2000

Designers: Flick, Book Design and Graphics
Simon Morse
Editor: Harriet Brown
Picture Researcher: Brian Hunter Smart

The author, Adrian Cooper, is an author and filmmaker who has worked in East Africa, India and, for Channel 4 and the BBC, in the UK.
The consultant, Rob Bowden, is an education consultant, author and photographer specialising in social and environmental issues.

A CIP catalogue record for this book is available from the British Library.

Dewey Classification: 382'.71

CONTENTS

INTRODUCTION

Trade routes have carried fabric, religion, food and music across the world for thousands of years. Today, our food, clothes and television programmes all arrive in our lives because of trade.

Trade that improves standards of living and benefits people is fair. Trade can create jobs and provide nations with wealth. This can be a huge benefit to people's lives. But trade can also be unfair. Unfair trade can ultimately deprive people of their basic human rights. This book sets out to answer some important questions. What is fair trade? Why is trade sometimes unfair? What can be done about it?

Trade can be exploitative. In some parts of the world, children are forced to do hard labour in terrible conditions. Very little of the money made by selling the goods actually reaches the workers.

4

Today, with fast and efficient internet connections, telephones and transport, it is easier than ever to communicate and trade with people all over the world.

GLOBALISATION OF TRADE

Today, people and goods can travel across the world quickly and easily. We can communicate across thousands of kilometres in a matter of seconds through emails and phone calls. Because of this, it has become very easy to trade with people across the world. This is called the globalisation of trade.

Globalisation is also changing the patterns of trade. We no longer have to get our food from a local farmer or grower. Food travels in refrigerated lorries, ships and aeroplanes so it arrives fresh from anywhere in the world. Companies move their offices or operations to parts of the world where labour is cheaper. For example, some companies have moved their call centres and customer support from the UK to India in order to save money.

TRADE IS NOT A NEW THING

People have always traded with each other. Back in Roman times, the ancient Silk Road linked the Chinese and Roman civilisations. It allowed silk to travel 6,500 km from China to Europe. Wool, gold and silver moved east from Europe into China. Across the Indian Ocean and Erythraean Sea (now the Red Sea), Swahili and Arabic traders used the wind to guide boats from Indonesia and the Indian sub-continent to Africa and then Arabia, bearing spices, ivory and precious stones. Even the Islamic cultures of east Africa began with trade, as did the movement of the Islamic faith and music to west Africa, along trade routes that criss-crossed the Sahara desert.

People have traded with each other for thousands of years. Today's global trade has caused a new set of problems.

TRADE WORDS

Trade – To exchange, buy or sell goods and services.

Goods – Anything that is made, farmed or mined, like clothes, food, oil and steel.

Services – A service is something that is provided such as banking, healthcare and communications.

Imports – Goods or services that arrive from another country.

Exports – Goods or services that are sent to another country.

Judging fairness

How do we measure the fairness of trade when we unwrap a brand new pair of shoes or a mobile phone? What if we find out the people involved in making our new shoes or phone were treated badly? Is this fair? What if we then find out the same people would be even worse off if they didn't have jobs at all?

These are difficult questions to keep asking and answering in our daily lives. But the globalisation of trade means that more and more governments, companies and individuals are involved and must themselves judge how fair their trade is. More than ever before, our lives are closely linked to people all over the world whose livelihoods depend on how fair trade is.

5

What's in a phone?

Everyday items that you probably take for granted exist because of trade. To make a mobile phone, you need raw materials sourced from many different parts of the world. Mobile phones contain plastics and metals including coltan, silicon, copper, gold, palladium, platinum and nickel. A mobile phone has a long journey from its raw materials to being sold in a shop in your local shopping centre.

WHY IS FAIR TRADE IMPORTANT?

One-fifth of the world's population do not have access to basic needs. There are one and a half billion people with inadequate shelter, over a billion people without access to safe water and 800 million people who are undernourished. Poverty isn't just about how much money people earn, it is also about access to education, jobs and healthcare. The outcomes of poverty – greater vulnerability and a lack of opportunities – are the same throughout the world. But how can fair trade help?

Millions of people across the world live in desperate poverty.

TRADING OUT OF POVERTY

Trade can generate investment, create job opportunities and lead to better education and healthcare facilities. It can put more money directly into a person's pocket so they can afford basic needs. Trade can be a way out of poverty. The average person in South Korea is nine times richer than they were 35 years ago. Over the same time period, South Korea's exports rose from just two and a half per cent of the whole economy to forty-two per cent of the economy.

Some people argue that helping a country to trade is more effective at reducing poverty than foreign aid donations. Foreign aid is often a short-term solution. Unfortunately, aid donations are sometimes accessible to corrupt government officials who can leave a population without any of the potential benefits. The revenue generated from trade is also far greater than the donations other countries might be willing to give.

If Africa, South America and south-east Asia all increased exports by one per cent, 128 million people could be lifted out of poverty.

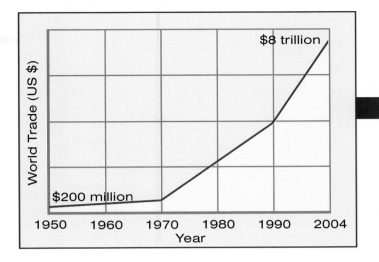

Since the Second World War, global trade has grown massively. Some countries have benefited from this, but many poor countries have been left behind. Millions of people still live in poverty.

GROWTH IN GLOBAL TRADE

The amount being traded globally has increased dramatically in the last 50 years. Since the Second World War ended in 1945, trade has created higher living standards for people in many regions of the world, including western Europe, Japan, Australia and North America. More goods and services are now being traded than at any other time in history. Today, global exports are worth over US $8 trillion per year. As trade increases, so does the wealth of individuals, companies and nations.

Miracle growth

A nation that has recently experienced 'miracle' growth because of trade is China. Every year between 1980 and 2000, China's economy grew by an average of ten per cent per year. Today, at least one-quarter of the world's toys are made and exported by China, as well as one-eighth of the world's clothes and footwear. This has led to the average Chinese person earning six times more than they did 20 years ago.

7

Unequal benefit

Although global trade and wealth is growing, not everybody has benefited. Over one billion people still survive on less than US $1 a day. This level of poverty means that nearly 11 million young children die each year before their fifth birthday from preventable illnesses, such as measles and diarrhoea.

Developing countries are trading more than ever before. Countries like China, Bangladesh and Mexico have experienced a particularly fast growth in trade. However, although Mexico is fast becoming a world leader in manufacturing and exporting technology, the benefit is not as great as it should be. Most of the financial benefit earned from Mexico's manufacturing ends up with the companies and individuals who sell the electronic goods to the consumers.

This is because the value of an electronic item in a Mexican factory is far less than its value when it is boxed and ready to be sold in a shop. This increase in a product's value, from factory to shop, is referred to as 'value added'. The value added to the item reflects the money used for paying people to make the item, parts, packaging, transport and advertising.

The growth of global trade has resulted in many environmental problems. The environment must be protected from the effects of global trade.

ENVIRONMENTAL COSTS

Global trade needs fuel: factories, cars, aeroplanes, ships and trucks don't run without oil and other fossil fuels. An increase in trade means an increase in the use of these fuels, which will run out one day. The world is using 70 per cent more energy than it was 30 years ago.

What is poverty?

Poverty is hunger. Poverty is lack of shelter. Poverty is being sick and not being able to see a doctor. Poverty is not being able to go to school. Poverty is not having a job, is fearing for the future and living one day at a time. Poverty is powerlessness, lack of representation and freedom. To alleviate poverty, developing economies need to grow faster, and the poor need to benefit from this growth. Trade can play an important part in reducing poverty because it boosts economic growth, which in turn benefits the poor.

(Source: World Bank)

Global warming

According to the World Wide Fund for Nature (WWF), 700 tonnes of carbon dioxide are pumped into the Earth's atmosphere every second, much of it as a by-product of global trading. To make matters worse, activities associated with trade are also depleting the world's forests and woodlands that would normally soak up carbon dioxide. A build-up of carbon dioxide in the atmosphere could lead to global climate change. If trade continues to increase, and measures are not put in place to protect the environment, the impact on our planet and on us, could be devastating.

A trade in humans

The Atlantic slave trade began in the late 1400s. People were sold at markets in east and west Africa and shipped to the Americas. At least one million people died from disease as they crossed the Atlantic in cramped boats.

When the survivors arrived on the other side of the Atlantic, conditions weren't much better. They were forced to work on cotton, tobacco, rice or sugar plantations in the Caribbean, Brazil and what is now the US.

In total, up to 28 million people were taken from their homes to work as slaves. The slave trade was finally abolished in the mid 1800s.

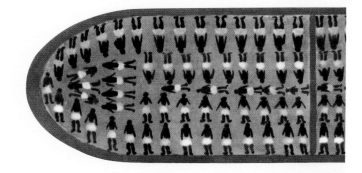

8

THE GLOBAL SUPERMARKET

The next time you walk along the aisles of a supermarket, imagine you're travelling across the world. The shelves of most shops are filled with foods from every continent and corner of the globe: chocolate from Ghana, cereal from Mexico, bananas from the West Indies, tomatoes from Spain. Because the supply of food you eat is now global, much of it travels thousands of kilometres before it arrives on your plate. But do the people who produce this food in the first place get a fair deal? And do you have any say in it?

The food you buy at a supermarket comes from all over the world.

SUPERMARKETS

Supermarket chains dominate the supply of food across the globe. Supermarkets have grown because they are able to use their power to negotiate good, if not always fair, deals. This trading power has allowed them to offer us low prices. As a result, supermarkets often do not pay their suppliers a fair price.

Where do we fit in?

We are all consumers. Every day of our lives, we consume different products. We eat a bowl of cereal, buy a pair of shoes, drink a cup of hot chocolate or watch a television programme. We can influence how things are traded in the global economy.

This is called 'consumer power'. Each time we buy something, we're telling the people who supply a product that we like it, need it or want it in our lives. Because we have consumer power, it means that we can influence whether or not things are fairly traded.

CHOCOLATE

However you consume chocolate – whether you eat a chocolate bar or have a hot or cold chocolate drink – it always begins life as a cocoa bean. Chocolate was first used to make a spicy drink in the Mayan civilisation in South America nearly 2,000 years ago. Today, chocolate is big business. Companies like Cadbury Schweppes, M&M/Mars, Hershey and Rowntree dominate what we see on the supermarket shelves. Almost two million tonnes of cocoa is produced every year. The world's largest grower of cocoa is the Ivory Coast in west Africa, which produces over half of the world's cocoa. So does the world trade in cocoa benefit the Ivory Coast?

Bitter taste of the chocolate trade

Towards the end of the 1990s, a United Nations (UN) report revealed that some Ivory Coast farmers enslaved children to work on cocoa fields. The US government reported that thousands of children between the ages of eight and twelve had been forced to work on farms that produced cocoa. Newspaper reports and television programmes claimed that the children worked in poor or dangerous conditions. Human rights organisations called this type of cocoa farming a modern-day example of the slave trade. Young people – some only eleven years old – spoke of being beaten and badly paid. Some of these children had been trafficked from countries like Burkina Faso and Mali, also in west Africa. Because the US imports over US $240 million worth of cocoa from the Ivory Coast every year, some of the chocolate consumed in the US is likely to be linked to child labour.

A bigger picture

At the same time as the reports of child labour in the Ivory Coast were made public, worldwide cocoa prices were at an all-time low. The Ivory Coast's prime minister said that it was partly the fault of large chocolate companies that child labour was used to produce cocoa. He argued that to stop child labour, companies would have to pay farmers a better price for cocoa.

As cocoa is often the only source of income for cocoa farmers, it is important that companies pay a fair price for it.

Unstable prices

Cocoa is the only source of income for many farmers in the Ivory Coast. When prices were low, people couldn't even afford to put food on the table. Today, cocoa prices have returned to normal. West African governments and chocolate companies have promised to work together to end child labour. Nevertheless, there are still reports of child labour in west Africa.

The price you pay for a jar of coffee is split between the grower, the exporter, the shipper and roaster, and the retailer. The diagram below shows how much each group receives. You can see how little the grower receives.

Exporter gets 10%

Coffee grower gets 10%

Retailer gets 25%

Shipper and roaster get 55%

THE PRICE OF COFFEE

The price of coffee beans changes daily. Like the price of all goods, the price of coffee is determined by how much supply is available and how much consumer demand there is. If there are more coffee beans harvested one year, the increase in supply will bring prices down. Whereas if consumers start drinking more coffee, the demand increases and raises the price of coffee. These trends are known as the 'law of supply and demand'. Between 2000 and 2004, coffee prices fell by over fifty per cent. This is mainly because more countries are producing coffee than ever before. World coffee supply has increased so the price of coffee has gone down. Farmers in developing countries are finding it harder than ever to cover the cost of basic needs and the livelihood of 25 million coffee producers around the world is under threat.

GOVERNMENT PROTECTION

It is not just developing countries that suffer from unfair trade. The wellbeing of any country depends on the supply of food. That's why the governments of the European Union (EU) made an agreement called the Common Agricultural Policy (CAP). This aimed to guarantee a minimum price for farmers and was achieved by offering them subsidies. Subsidies are quantities of money which are offered to farmers to help them grow a particular crop.

Is it fair?

European governments spend a total of £30 billion on agricultural subsidies every year. But not all farmers benefit from government support. Though 40 per cent of farms in Europe are small farms, they only account for eight per cent of agricultural production and so only receive eight per cent of government subsidies. Large farms get more money than small farms; so they are able to buy new, efficient equipment and can produce food more cheaply. Farmers with large farms win two-fold and farmers with small farms lose out.

11

MILK LAKES AND SUGAR MOUNTAINS

Dairy farms in Europe receive billions of dollars from EU governments to produce milk and related products like butter, yoghurt and powdered milk. This is the equivalent of every cow in Europe getting US $2 a day. Farmers are guaranteed to receive a certain price for what they produce, even if people in Europe don't want to consume the products. This leads to the over-production of milk in Europe. This surplus can be sold on the world market very cheaply. EU countries also produce a large amount of sugar. In 2003, they sold 4.8 million tonnes of sugar on the world market. Some of this sugar is sold for a much lower price on the world market than it's sold for locally. But is this fair?

Dumping

When the surplus of a product is sold cheaply on the open market, it is called 'dumping'. Dumping forces down the prices paid to producers all over the world. Sugar farms in Mozambique were forced to compete by cutting costs so they got rid of staff. These unemployed people spent less and other areas of the economy suffered. In a country like Mozambique, which relies heavily on sugar, the impact of dumping can ripple out to trap an entire nation in poverty.

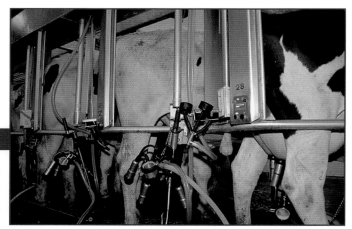

EU dumping can have devastating consequences for countries whose economies rely on the income from just one or two products or crops.

12

Lunchtime in England

The next time you have a meal, take a look at your plate and think about where your food has actually come from. For just one meal, your food could have travelled thousands of kilometres!

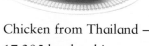

Potatoes from Italy – 2,447 km by lorry

Chicken from Thailand – 17,205 km by ship

Broccoli from Zambia – 7,900 km by plane

Carrots from Spain – 1,610 km by lorry

Cabbage from Britain – 200 km by lorry

Peas from Zimbabwe – 8,255 km by plane

From the port to the supermarket – 1,585 km. Total = 39,202 km

(Source: Sustain)

FAIR TRADE IN CLOTHES?

Clothing the world is worth US $350 billion a year. It is not surprising that fashion companies like Gucci, Versace and Burberry draw attention to themselves with extravagant catwalk shows. Companies like GAP or Nike spend billions on advertising campaigns each year. One way of making sure consumers keep on buying is to keep prices as competitive as possible. To do this, fashion companies search for cheaper ways to produce clothes.

Relocate

Over the last 30 years, garment production has shifted from the UK and the US, for example, to places like China, Bangladesh, Cambodia and Sri Lanka. In these countries, people's wages tend to be much lower than in the UK and the US. Lower labour costs mean lower production costs. Companies are therefore able to keep the cost of their clothes lower and make more profit. This globalisation of manufacturing is now an important source of income for millions of people in poorer countries. However, workers in richer countries lose out as numerous factories are closed.

FASHION VICTIMS

Germany used to be the world's largest producer of textiles, but in the last 30 years, hundreds of thousands of people have lost their jobs. In the UK too, employment in the clothing and textile industry has fallen from over one million to 200,000 in the same time period. Marks & Spencer – one of the UK's biggest retailers – used to source 90 per cent of its clothes from the UK. Now their clothes are manufactured outside Europe, from Morocco to south-east Asia, providing a boost for the economy of these countries.

Too long for too little

Today, the world's leading producer of textiles and fashion is China. But some Chinese factory workers complain of unhealthy and unsafe working conditions. Workers producing sportswear in a Chinese factory often work seven days a week during the peak seasons. And it isn't just China. The sewing department in one Indonesian factory had to work a 21-hour shift to complete a last minute order from a well-known sportswear label. Under the pressure of

Clothing manufacture in Europe used to be big business. In the last 30 years, hundreds of mills and factories have closed down.

tight deadlines, many factories around the world reportedly force workers to do overtime. In many cases, despite working long hours, many employees still don't earn enough to support their families.

'Stupid. Lazy. Useless.'

Verbal abuse by factory bosses has been reported in clothing factories. There are even cases of physical abuse and sexual harassment. In many cases, workers are employed on short-term contracts. This makes it difficult for the workers to complain as it's easy for a factory to dismiss contract workers. There is also a constant stream of people waiting to fill any vacant positions. To make it even more difficult to protest, trade unions, who look after the interests of the employees, are not encouraged in many factories and are often forbidden.

People working in clothing and textile factories are sometimes treated badly and made to work long shifts for little pay.

14

Chemical dyes and pesticides

Reports from eastern Europe and south-east Asia often describe poor health amongst factory workers. Eye damage, back pain, allergies and respiratory disease aren't unusual. Some dye powders and liquids used for dyeing textiles, paper and leather can cause serious health problems. A dye called benzidine has been linked to bladder cancer in people who are in regular contact with it. In 2003, the EU countries banned some chemical dyes because of health concerns.

In west Africa, farmers growing cotton for the manufacture of jeans and T-shirts suffer regular illnesses linked to pesticides. Some farmers can't afford to buy the protective face masks and gloves recommended by the pesticide manufacturers. Every year, up to 20,000 deaths in poorer nations are linked to the use of agricultural pesticides.

Cotton is woven into fabric in factories all over the world. Workers aren't always well-treated.

TWO COTTON COUNTRIES

In the US, cotton farmers are guaranteed to get a good price for their cotton. All 25,000 cotton farmers receive subsidies from the government. In fact, between 2001 and 2002, the US government spent US $4 billion on cotton subsidies. This is more than the value of the cotton itself when sold on the open market. Subsidies allow US farmers to sell cotton at very low prices without losing profit.

Benin, in west Africa, also grows and trades in cotton. This trade has contributed to the growth of Benin's economy. Profits from cotton have contributed to new schools, roads and healthcare facilities. However, there are no government subsidies in Benin, so if farmers want to sell their cotton, they have to cut their prices to match those of the US cotton farmers.

If the US didn't subsidise its farmers so heavily, Benin cotton farmers could make a better living and contribute more to the economy of their country. US cotton subsidies are so great that, incredibly, they are worth twice the value of Benin's entire economy.

Sick man of Europe

When ships, locomotives and industries ran on coal, south Wales produced a third of the total world coal exports. Today, these coal industries have gone. Unemployment and poor living conditions have depressed the coal communities of Wales ever since. In 2000, the EU invested £1.2 billion into Wales to revive the economies of the mining valleys.

15

ELECTRONICS AND GEMS

The world consumes a growing variety of electronics – better quality flat television screens, cheaper computers, broadband internet connections in people's homes and satellite navigation in cars. There are already over a billion television households, over a billion mobile phone users and 600 million internet users. The future will definitely be smaller, lighter and faster when it comes to electronics. But none of it will be possible without one important ingredient – tantalum.

FROM THE EARTH

Tantalum is the metal used in electronic circuit boards. Tantalum is refined from an ore called columbite-tantalite, or coltan. Coltan is so valuable that it's known as black gold.

Coltan rush

Extracted from mines in Australia, Brazil, the Democratic Republic of the Congo (DRC) and Canada, the worldwide supply of coltan is valued at over US $6 billion per year. Demand for electronics has made coltan more expensive. In 2000, the price went from US $65 per kg to US $600 per kg. This rise in price attracted tens of thousands of people to the Kahuzi Biega National Park in the DRC in central Africa. They came from within the DRC and from surrounding countries including Rwanda and Uganda. People came in search of the black gold. In central Africa, trade in coltan is often controlled by militia groups who buy illegal arms using the profits from coltan. In 2001, over US $30 million a month was being made from illegal coltan mining in the DRC. Most of it was used to fund a bloody conflict that began in the mid-1990s.

Coltan is extracted legally from mines in Australia, Brazil and Canada. But in the Democratic Republic of the Congo, coltan is being used to finance a bloody civil war.

Gorillas pay the price

Over the last few decades, central Africa has suffered a lot of violence which has resulted in the movement of a large number of people. The most important national parks were already under pressure from this movement, and the coltan rush has put further pressure on the wildlife and natural environment in this region. Forests have been cleared, rivers contaminated and gorillas living on the lowlands have been killed and sold as 'bushmeat' in local markets. In 1994, the gorilla population was 17,000. There are now fewer than 5,000 eastern lowland gorillas left.

Safety

It wasn't just the gorillas in central Africa that suffered. Because mining coltan in national parks is illegal, safety is largely ignored. In February 2002, 36 coltan miners were killed when an excavated riverbank collapsed on them.

'Blood on your handset'

Activists, supported by movie star Leonardo Di Caprio and the author Arthur C Clarke, made the headlines protesting about coltan from central Africa. Mobile phone companies quickly issued statements stating that they didn't use coltan from the region. In reality, it's hard to tell where coltan shipments come from, as they pass through many traders before being used in electronic circuits.

The trade in diamonds is also surrounded by conflict and controversy (see page 18).

17

Central Africa has suffered decades of violence. Many people have been forced from their homes. Now the natural environment is also under threat from coltan mining.

CITY OF GEMS

Ratnapura means 'City of Gems' in Sinhalese, the main language of Sri Lanka. Eighty per cent of blue sapphires traded worldwide come from Sri Lanka. Their export of gemstones is worth US $90 million and employs 175,000 people. Yet, this wealth does not reach the majority of the population because there's more money to be had selling sapphires then digging for them. Forty per cent of the people in Ratnapura live in poverty.

In 2003, 120,000 people were displaced from their homes and 61 people died because of flooding. Local experts believe the flooding was caused by illegal gem mining. If Sri Lanka's government and the sapphire selling community don't take steps to control illegal digging, it won't be long before more people are drowned in the swelling rivers of Sri Lanka.

CONFLICT DIAMONDS

Diamonds may be a sign of love or luxury, but some are called 'conflict diamonds'. Conflict diamonds come from areas controlled by military groups who are opposed to their government. Conflict diamonds are used to buy weapons which are then used in civil wars, particularly in west and central Africa. Militia groups in Angola and Sierra Leone control the trade of uncut diamonds, smuggling them through neighbouring African countries. Conflict diamonds are often used for industrial purposes, but some end up in the jewellery shops of EU and US cities.

Most conflict diamonds come from Sierra Leone, Angola, Liberia and the DRC. Citizens have been terrorized, mutilated and killed by groups in control of the local illegal diamond trade. Some conflict diamonds end up being sold in jewellers in developed countries.

The wages that are paid to people who dig for gemstones are a tiny proportion of the value added to expensive jewellery sold in shops all over the world.

FAIR TRADE IN ARMS?

In July 2003, mortar bombs fell on the civilian population in Monrovia, the capital of Liberia in west Africa. Some of the mortars were launched by child soldiers only eleven years old. The mortars had been built in Iran and then illegally supplied by the government of Guinea, a country that borders Liberia to the north. The trade in illegal arms is born out of the huge legal production of weapons throughout the world. Problems arise when these legal arms end up in the wrong hands.

ILLEGAL ARMS

Profits made from the trade in illegal arms encourage further illegal activities. Kidnapping in Colombia, murder in Iraq or gun crime in London often involve illegal weapons. Technological advances such as mobile phones, faster internet access and more powerful computers make trade quicker and easier. Although this is beneficial when the products are legal, it can be very undesirable when the trade is in an illegal weapon.

Each year, US $30 billion worth of legal arms are sold. It is quite possible that some of these arms will ultimately end up in the wrong hands.

Weapons and war

In western Sudan in 2004, an armed militia known as 'Janjaweed' launched attacks on civilians. They set fire to villages and terrorised, raped and killed many people. Over a million people have fled their homes in the Darfur, a region the size of France or Texas, and are now living in terrible conditions in refugee camps. EU countries and the US have an arms embargo on Sudan, which means that they do not supply Sudan with arms. But despite this, weapons are widely available.

As the Cold War drew to an end – following the collapse of the Berlin Wall in 1989 – there were huge stockpiles of weapons across central and eastern Europe. In 2002, the Czech government announced that it had sold 95,000 small arms, 200 tanks and 50 aeroplanes since 1993. The Ukraine sold 330,000 sub-machine guns. In 1994, some of these weapons were used to kill up to one million people in Rwanda's horrific genocide.

Access to small arms has increased all over the world because of uncontrolled arms sales. As trade in arms increases, whether it be legal or illegal, the price of weapons drops. More people can then afford to arm themselves, often with terrible consequences.

LEGAL ARMS

It isn't just old or illegal weapons that circulate the world. In the last 40 years, the number of countries manufacturing arms has doubled and eight million small arms are

Legal weapons can end up in a country that may use them against innocent civilians.

now made each year. Billions of dollars are made from the trade in legal arms every year and although they are sold legally, it is often difficult to know where they end up. It is usual for parts of weapons to be sold, rather than whole weapons. This makes tracing them even more difficult. A recent report showed that arms parts from Britain were reaching countries like Zimbabwe, Israel, Colombia and Uganda. It is illegal for British companies to export complete weapons to these countries because such countries are involved in activities that deprive people of their basic human rights.

Legal loopholes

The Canadian government has a good reputation for not trading with countries who have a poor human rights record. Despite this, 33 Canadian helicopters ended up in Colombia – a country with a history of human rights abuse. A legal loophole allowed the helicopters to be sold in the US first, then onto Colombia. Even if a country sells arms legally, it can be impossible to guarantee where those arms will eventually be used.

20

What if...?

• In 1999, South Africa spent US $6 billion buying submarines, aircraft, helicopters and naval ships. If they'd spent the money on HIV/AIDS treatment, it could have paid for the medicine to treat five million people for two years.

• If governments halved their spending on arms and the military, every single child throughout the world would be able to go through primary education.

FAIR TRADE IN MEDICINE?

We often take it for granted that when we fall sick we can get medicine to help us get better. But many people in developing countries can't afford this luxury.

No-one likes being ill – but sickness is a part of our lives. When we're ill we can buy medicine from a local pharmacy, visit our doctor or get treatment at a nearby hospital. Not everyone in the world has access to this kind of medical treatment. One-third of the world's population – that's almost two billion people – don't have regular access to affordable medicine. Poverty and a lack of healthcare facilities within a country contribute to the problem. So, too, does the price of medicine itself.

TOO EXPENSIVE

Forty million people around the world are infected with HIV/AIDS. Three million are under the age of fifteen. Up to five million people were infected in 2003 alone, while three million died of AIDS-related illnesses in the same year. The medicine to suppress HIV/AIDS can cost US $15,000 a year per person.

In South Africa, five million people are infected with HIV/AIDS – that's one in every nine people. But if the average yearly income in South Africa is around US $10,000, how are the people with HIV/AIDS supposed to afford the drugs?

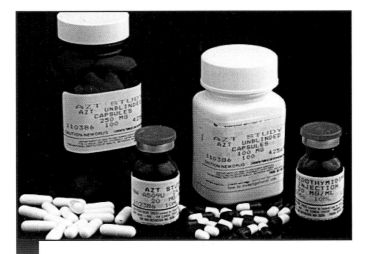

Medicines can be very expensive. Often, they are beyond the reach of those that need them the most.

It is possible to produce cheap, copycat medicines. But this can create problems both for those that sell the drug, and those that buy it.

Cheaper medicine

An Indian company called Cipla can make HIV/AIDS medicine for US $350 per year. The company produces 'copycat' or 'generic' medicine. The medicine is almost exactly the same as the more expensive versions. More importantly, it means millions of people are able to afford HIV drugs. Cipla supplies South Africa with cheaper medicine. But in 2001, the South African government was taken to court for buying this generic medicine. Companies who own the original patent or copyright for producing the HIV/AIDS drugs said that Cipla and the South African government were acting illegally.

Future research

It costs pharmaceutical companies a lot of money to research and develop new medicines. It can cost over US $600 million dollars and take around 15 years to develop and produce a top patented drug. The pharmaceutical companies argue that patents are not

only about protecting their profit, but are there to make sure there is enough funding to go into the research of future medicines. What's more, there is an international trade law – known as TRIPS (see page 33) – that makes it illegal to copy medicines.

Although it is expensive to make a drug, selling it makes a lot of money. The ten largest pharmaceutical companies earned a combined profit of US $35.9 billion in 2002. The US pharmaceutical companies alone earn billions of dollars from patented drugs, so it's not surprising that they want to stop 'pirates' copying their formulas and selling copycat medicine.

The biggest five pharmaceutical companies – Merck, Johnson & Johnson, Pfizer, GlaxoSmithKline and Novartis – often each make sales of over US $20 billion a year.

Copyright?

A global campaign was launched challenging the pharmaceutical companies.

International aid agencies such as Oxfam and Medecins Sans Frontieres, together with activist groups like Health GAP in the US, the Treatment Action Campaign in South Africa, and the Geneva-based Third World Network, argued that patent laws must not be a barrier to getting life-saving medicines to the millions in need. Partly in response to this pressure, pharmaceutical companies have dropped court cases to defend their patents (in South Africa, Brazil and Thailand). The global rules that protect public health over patent rights have been reinforced, providing legal and political strength for governments to get the most affordable treatments for people in need.

Essential medicine

The agreement to make cheap HIV/AIDS drugs available to those that need it the most was made in November 2001 during a world trade conference in Qatar, a country east of Saudi Arabia. Governments are now allowed to issue a 'compulsory license' when there is a 'public health crisis'. In other words, when an infectious disease is as widespread as HIV/AIDS, the government is allowed to buy cheaper, copycat medicine.

Bigger picture

The World Health Organisation (WHO) reported that most medical research done worldwide into new medicine is for the richest ten per cent of the world's population. There is a bigger profit selling Viagra than selling medicines for diseases like malaria or bilharzia, which are more widespread in the developing world. Out of 1,223 new medicines made between 1975 and 1997, only 13 were for tropical diseases widespread in developing countries.

Because of this problem, and the experience of the South African government being taken to court, Kofi Annan – the UN's Secretary General – said the world needed a global fund for medicine. This was the only way to make sure enough money was put into making medicine that pharmaceutical companies were less interested in making.

In 2002, the Global Health Fund was started. To be successful it needed between US $7 billion and US $10 billion. This is just a fraction of the rich countries' weapons budget, for example. But after two years, the Global Health Fund has received only US $2.6 billion. It is too little to allow the majority of the world's population to benefit from medical research and treatment.

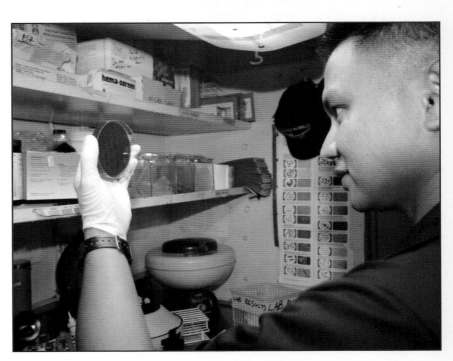

ILLEGAL DRUGS TRADE

There are over 50 million people worldwide who regularly use illegal drugs. The illegal drugs trade is estimated to be worth as much as global tourism – about US $400 billion a year. The governments of the world spend billions of dollars each year treating and rehabilitating addicts, combatting drug-related crime and trying to stop the illegal drugs trade.

Governments try to prevent drugs entering their country. Customs officials and the police are fighting the war on illegal drugs.

GLOBAL NETWORK

Like any other product traded across the world today, the globalisation of transport and communication means that illegal drugs move faster and more easily. In cars, planes, boats, by camel or on foot, heroin and opium travels from countries in the 'Golden Triangle' (Laos, Myanmar and Thailand) or the 'Golden Crescent' (Afghanistan, Pakistan and Iran) through central Asia and Europe. Cocaine is predominantly produced in South America. It is trafficked into the US and across the Atlantic towards Africa and Europe. Synthetic drugs, such as Ecstasy, are mainly made in Europe and are trafficked all over the world.

A crop like any other?

Coca – the raw material for cocaine – has been grown in South America for thousands of years. Coca leaves are sold for making coca tea (or 'Mate de Coca'). This tea is 'decocainised' and is legal to drink. However, the growth and export of coca as the drug cocaine is illegal. In Afghanistan, opium, which can be refined to make heroin, is the most lucrative crop a farmer can grow.

Some farmers grow drug crops because it is more lucrative than growing legal crops. Subsidies in Europe and the US have forced down the price of legal crops. If the subsidies were scrapped, poor farmers would have an incentive to grow legal crops rather than illegal drugs. Many farmers believe that governments should be responsible for their own people's addiction to illegal drugs. They feel it is not the responsibility of farmers, who have little choice of what to grow.

A BUSINESS LIKE ANY OTHER?

It's not unusual for drug traffickers and dealers to be arrested at airports or border crossings as they transport drugs to cities and towns across the world. But these people don't control the drugs trade. They are couriers in a secretive chain of 'middle-men', all organised by drug 'barons'.

Trading illegal drugs is a business like any other to drug barons. They employ highly qualified professionals to help maximise their profits. One Colombian cartel did 'market research' by testing their drug supplies on people in Puerto Rico before moving on to try the larger US market.

There is an increasing availability of illegal drugs in Vietnam. As a result there has been a rise in the levels of addiction amongst Vietnam's population.

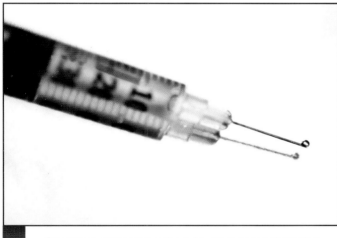

Sharing dirty needles is one way that the HIV virus is spread. By mid 2004, around 43.4 million people worldwide were living with HIV/AIDS .

Human cost

The drug trade destroys millions of lives every year. Whether it is murder committed between rival crack-cocaine gangs on the streets of New York, a heroin addict in Rome robbing another person's home to feed their habit, or families who watch their loved ones grapple with drug addiction in Tajikistan: millions suffer because of the illegal trade.

DECRIMINALISATION DEBATE

The HIV virus that leads to AIDS can be transmitted by sharing unclean needles. In Vietnam, two-thirds of the people infected with HIV/AIDS are drug users. Most are under the age of twenty-three. In Ho Chi Min City in Vietnam, 'professional' injectors supply thousands of people with heroin. In the process they spread the HIV virus.

The human and economic costs of illegal drugs have prompted people to question whether current measures to stop the illegal drug trade are working. It's argued that drug-related illness and crime would be reduced more quickly by relaxing laws that make drugs illegal. If legal pharmacists prescribed heroin to users, they wouldn't have to rely on the criminal underworld. Drug users could also have access to free, clean needles rather than using needles that may be infected with HIV. This could go some way to tackling the spread of HIV/AIDS around the world.

25

FAIR TRADE IN MONEY?

North America is one of the largest economies in the world. Investment is encouraged and its influence has spread throughout the world. The US mostly trades with South America, western Europe and east Asia.

Financial transactions travel via satellite in an instant. Investors can move money to any part of the world at the click of a button. Developing countries often rely on money from more wealthy countries and organisations. However, debt is a problem that affects many countries. What happens when a poor country can't pay back the money it owes?

NORTH AMERICA

South America is the most urbanized region in the developing world. Deep inequalities of wealth exist here. Exports are mainly to North America and Europe.

SOUTH AMERICA

FREE MOVEMENT OF MONEY

In the early 1990s, the governments of Thailand, Indonesia, South Korea and the Philippines made it easier for people from all over the world to invest in local businesses and industries. Foreign investment poured into south-east Asia and skyscrapers soon towered above Thailand's capital city, Bangkok. It looked like the free movement of money was helping Thailand's economy to grow.

Crisis in Thailand

What the new buildings didn't show was that Thailand's economy wasn't actually performing very well. When foreign investors realised there was a problem, one by one they began to withdraw from Thailand. The money that was able to move fast and freely into the country, left just as quickly. In 18 months, most of the foreign investment had disappeared. Investors became nervous about investing in the whole region and as a result the free movement of money turned an economic crisis in Thailand into a social disaster across south-east Asia.

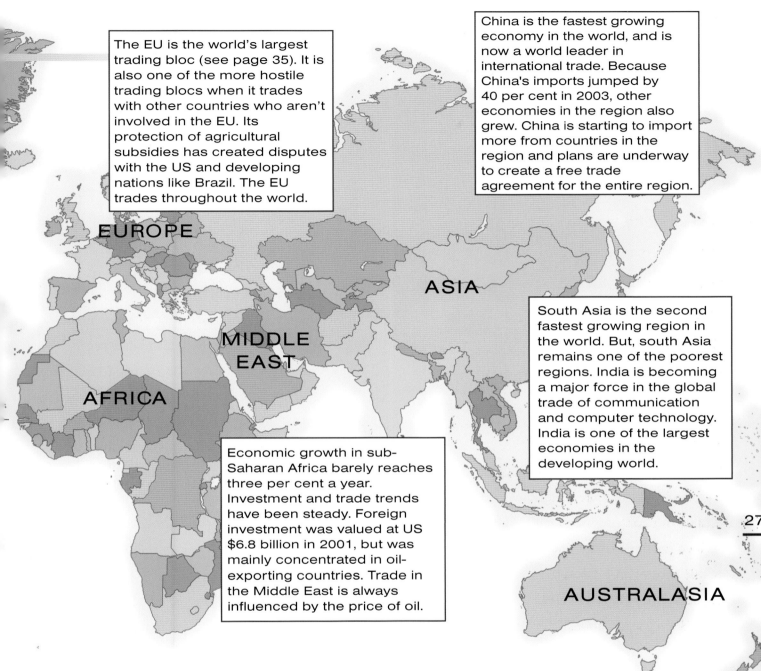

The EU is the world's largest trading bloc (see page 35). It is also one of the more hostile trading blocs when it trades with other countries who aren't involved in the EU. Its protection of agricultural subsidies has created disputes with the US and developing nations like Brazil. The EU trades throughout the world.

China is the fastest growing economy in the world, and is now a world leader in international trade. Because China's imports jumped by 40 per cent in 2003, other economies in the region also grew. China is starting to import more from countries in the region and plans are underway to create a free trade agreement for the entire region.

EUROPE

ASIA

MIDDLE EAST

South Asia is the second fastest growing region in the world. But, south Asia remains one of the poorest regions. India is becoming a major force in the global trade of communication and computer technology. India is one of the largest economies in the developing world.

AFRICA

Economic growth in sub-Saharan Africa barely reaches three per cent a year. Investment and trade trends have been steady. Foreign investment was valued at US $6.8 billion in 2001, but was mainly concentrated in oil-exporting countries. Trade in the Middle East is always influenced by the price of oil.

AUSTRALASIA

27

Gambling with lives?

By the end of 1998, there was mass unemployment and widespread depression across south-east Asia. Governments could no longer pay for important public services like health and education. In Indonesia, 20 million people became unemployed in under one year, 250,000 health clinics closed down and six million children dropped out of school. The south-east

Asian governments were given loans of US $120 billion to help their economies. Many south-east Asian countries are now thriving. However, the effects of the depression are still being felt in Indonesia. The violence there is often linked with the economic depression. It's hard to tell how long an economic crisis will last and how far it will spread.

In December 2001, tens of thousands of people took to the streets of Argentina to demand the removal of the corrupt politicians who had driven Argentina into poverty.

ARGENTINA'S CRISIS

During the second half of the 20th century, Argentina was run by corrupt governments who handled the economy very badly. They caused massive unemployment and threw Argentina into a terrible recession. Fifteen million people were forced to live in near poverty.

Riots in the streets

In late 2001, the government, which was in massive debt, failed to pay a US $132 billion loan repayment. They told the people of Argentina that they couldn't withdraw more than US $800 a month from their own bank accounts. People were angry and worried about losing their life's savings so they took to the streets to try to get rid of the president, Fernando de la Rua, and all those that were corrupt within the government. Public demonstrations, looting and riots left 27 people dead.

A new start?

By the beginning of 2002, the president of Argentina had been replaced five times in just two weeks. The fifth president, Eduardo Duhalde, restored some calm but it wasn't until Nestor Kirchner became president in 2003 that Argentina really started along the road to reform. By 2004, the violence and protests had all but died out but there is still the ongoing problem of the massive, unpayed loans.

Why were they in debt?

South American countries borrowed money in the 1960s and 1970s in order to industrialise their countries. This is what led to the current debt crisis. The first signs of the crisis appeared in 1982 when the Mexican government announced that it could no longer repay what it had borrowed from foreign banks and governments. The experience of Argentina, Brazil and Uruguay show that old debts continue to cause problems for developing nations today.

The depth of debt

Between 1990 and 1997, the poorest nations of the world paid US $77 billion more to repay old debts than they received in new bank loans. On average, countries in Africa spend US $40 million every day towards paying back debts. Because so much is spent on repaying old debt, less is available to spend on essential health and education facilities.

FREE TRADE DISPUTES

Free trade means there are no 'barriers' stopping the movement of goods or services in and out of a country. Governments use barriers like tariffs or subsidies to protect a nation's industries from foreign imports. Tariffs are sums of money that are added to products entering the country. This means that they become more expensive for people to buy. If a government 'opens up' for trade, it means it reduces these barriers to encourage the free movement of goods and services.

Governments try to protect their industries by putting tariffs onto foreign imports.

OPEN WORLD

Since the Second World War, international organisations have been created that support and encourage open trade between nations. The International Monetary Fund (IMF), World Bank and World Trade Organisation (WTO) have become very powerful forces in the global economy.

Bank loans

The IMF was set up to create stability in the international economy. The IMF lends money to governments. The World Bank also lends money, but is involved in longer-term projects like building new factories, roads and water supplies, or improving education and healthcare. Both the IMF and World Bank give much needed loans to countries throughout the world. In return for the loans, countries are asked to take certain steps to encourage

free trade. During the 1990s, countries that needed to borrow money only qualified if they agreed to make 'structural adjustments'. These adjustments involved removing subsidies and tariffs. Foreign imports grew, local industries couldn't compete and then closed down. Because of this and other associated problems, the adjustments have been blamed for making the debt crisis worse in many developing countries, including Zimbabwe and Kenya.

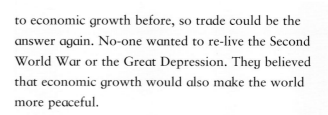

A century of trade

The 19th century was a period of enormous economic growth in western Europe and the US. The standard of living improved and nations became wealthier. The French economy grew so much in the 1890s that it is known as 'la belle époque', or the good old days. One of the main forces behind this great transformation in people's lives was trade.

In the 19th century, trade helped to improve the standard of living in western Europe and the US.

The Great Depression

When the US stock market in Wall Street collapsed one day in 1929, the social and economic depression that followed lasted ten years. At the time, nations reacted by protecting their local industries from competition by other companies. They used tariffs to restrict trade which made relations between countries very hostile.

Never again

At the end of the Second World War, the governments of Europe and the US needed to rebuild war-torn countries. Trade had led to economic growth before, so trade could be the answer again. No-one wanted to re-live the Second World War or the Great Depression. They believed that economic growth would also make the world more peaceful.

New international organisations

Towards the end of the Second World War, 28 countries met in a small US town called Bretton Woods. Here, they started to design international organisations that would rebuild countries after the war, and help the global economy become more stable in the future. The International Monetary Fund (IMF) and the World Bank were the first of these international organisations to be set up.

Free trade organisation

A series of meetings about international trade began in 1947. Called the General Agreement on Tariffs and Trade (GATT), the main aim was to create trade rules to stop the protective trade tactics that had caused hostile international relations during the Great Depression. The last major GATT meetings took place between 1986 and 1994 in Uruguay. This 'Uruguay round' led to a permanent organisation called the World Trade Organisation (WTO).

30

In Seattle, 1999, a WTO meeting discussed trading rules. It failed to agree on many issues.

DISPUTES

Once a country becomes a member of the WTO, it agrees to trade according to various WTO rules. If member countries have a disagreement about trade, the WTO uses the trade rules to settle disputes. The WTO has resolved trade deadlocks, but it has faced criticism for rules that don't always benefit free and fair trade.

Does free trade mean fair trade?

In 1999, a WTO discussion in the US city of Seattle was forced to end early. Up to 50,000 people had gathered in protest outside the WTO meeting. This was a major event in the 'anti-globalisation' or 'anti-capitalist' movement. People from around the world protested about many issues: the environment, animal rights, sweatshops, and debt in developing countries. The WTO was accused of being too secretive in the way it settled trade disputes. People argued that meetings should include organisations other than government representatives, such as trade unions, environmental groups and human rights organisations. They also argued that the WTO should be more democratic and operate a system of 'one country one vote', instead of 'one dollar one vote'.

World Trade Organisation
The WTO has permanent headquarters in Geneva, Switzerland. Since it started in 1995, 147 countries have become members. The WTO's goal is to promote free trade and economic growth using a system of trade rules that have been steadily developed since the Second World War in a series of discussions or 'trade rounds'. Rules discussed and created during trade rounds relate to all goods and services, including food and clothes, electronic equipment and medicine. No matter what is being traded, every rule is meant to encourage free trade.

31

ANJIN HEJU
PANAMA

CANCUN, 2003

Four years after Seattle, another WTO meeting failed. The meeting was being held in Cancun, Mexico. It was part of the series of discussions called the 'Doha round', named after the city in the Middle East where the trade talks started in 2001.

Although there were demonstrations on the streets of Cancun, bigger disputes happened inside the meeting itself. West African countries like Ghana, Burkina Faso and Benin complained of unfair cotton subsidies. The US argued that factory workers employed in textile and steel industries

US steel workers are losing jobs because of changes in world trade.

were losing jobs because of changes in world trade and EU tariffs. India and China criticised the WTO's rules on the movement of global money and access to technology. While on the streets outside the conference, a farmer called Lee Kyoung-Hae took his own life. He was the head of a group of farmers from South Korea that were protesting about being forced out of business because of rice dumping.

Trade talks collapse

The WTO meeting suddenly ended on 14th September, 2003, when groups of people representing the African countries walked out. They argued that developing countries were being pressured into opening up their economies to free trade by richer countries who were not prepared to do the same. They accused richer nations of double standards, by using subsidies and tariffs that made it more difficult for developing countries to access global markets.

End of a 'rich man's club'?

Some people celebrated the collapse of the Cancun talks. They saw it as a victory for poorer nations. It was the first time India, Brazil and China, three vast countries with massive populations, had stood side-by-side on certain issues to create an alliance that challenged the EU and US. They argued that the collapse of talks had broken years of WTO decisions that had favoured richer countries. They accused the WTO of being a club that helps richer nations instead of serving free and fair trade.

Keep talking

Others were bitterly disappointed when the talks ended in Cancun. They argued that if WTO rounds continue to fail in the future, fair trade debates will not be solved. If these debates are not solved, then neither rich nor poor nations will benefit. They argued that governments need the WTO so they can improve controversial trade rules and stop trade wars (see pages 35-36).

Controversial WTO trade rules:

TRIPS

TRIPS – or Trade-Related Aspects of Intellectual Property Rights – are rules which aim to protect investments that companies make researching and developing new ideas that improve technology, medicine and biotechnology. TRIPS also protect artists and authors from having their music, books or films copied. TRIPS can make medicines and technology more expensive for poorer nations. Access to technology in developing countries becomes more difficult when extra copyright costs have to be met by small businesses. China and India argue that TRIPS creates a 'technology gap' that slows down economic development and makes global trade unfair. TRIPS has been successfully challenged. Pharmaceutical companies took the South African government to court when it supplied copycat HIV/AIDS drugs to its people. The TRIPS rules were overturned in favour of public health (see pages 21-23).

MAI

In 1995, several large companies in developed countries approached the WTO with a request to make it easier for companies to invest in other parts of the world. The Multilateral Agreement on Investment (MAI) was designed to give global corporations more power when they invested in foreign countries. If the WTO agreed to MAI, it would mean governments would have to compensate anyone who was not able to invest freely.

The WTO was supposed to make a decision about MAI by 1998. Before this deadline, a campaign based on the internet criticised the aims of MAI. Because of the campaign, the governments of France, USA and Australia questioned the legal power that MAI would give to companies. They were concerned that companies would gain too much power, and even become as powerful as the governments themselves. The MAI deadline came and went without any decision, but it is possible that it could resurface one day.

GATS

Services like banking, healthcare and communication are covered by the General Agreement on Trade in Services (GATS). The idea of GATS is to make it easier for private companies to invest in service industries. Foreign investment can provide technology and skills, which can lower prices and improve services. Allowing profit-motivated private companies from other countries to run essential services like water, health and education can also increase prices and reduce the quality of services. This is what happened in Bolivia, in 2000, when a US company called Bechtel started running the water supply in the city of Cochabamba. Water became so expensive that it cost nearly a third of people's income. It was even illegal to collect rainwater as any falling water was the property of Bechtel. Violent demonstrations spread across the city, and Bechtel pulled out. Later, a French water company successfully privatised the water supply in the city of La Paz, the capital of Bolivia, by allowing people to pay for improvements by contributing their labour rather than money.

33

DROP THE DEBT

The World Bank and IMF have also been criticised by the governments of developing countries and anti-globalisation protesters. They argue that the adjustments that poorer nations were asked to undertake to qualify for bank loans had deepened debt.

In 1996, the World Bank and IMF decided to reduce the burden of foreign debt repayments in 42 countries. These countries were referred to as 'Highly Indebted Poor Countries' (HIPC). An agreement was reached between the World Bank, the IMF, richer nations and other debt relief programmes to cancel US $100 billion worth of HIPC debt over several years.

But is it working?

A campaign started in 1996 by an organisation called Jubilee 2000 argued that the debt relief process was too slow and that more countries should have their debt cancelled.

Although by 2003 over US $18 billion had been cancelled by the HIPC project, according to Jubilee 2000, 13 out of 20 countries will not have their debts lowered to a level that is sustainable.

However, the debt relief that has been granted is working. In ten African countries receiving debt relief under the HIPC project, education spending increased by US $1.3 billion in 2002. There has also been in an increase in spending on healthcare. Debt relief is a long and drawn-out process but it is a step in the right direction.

Many developing countries would benefit from the cancellation of debt. This would free up more money which could be used for education and to alleviate poverty.

TRADE WARS

In the same way that the WTO aims to encourage international free trade, countries often sign agreements between each other for the same reason. These agreements are sometimes called 'trade blocs'. Though trade inside these regional or international blocs is more open, there have been an increasing number of disputes between trade blocs, known as trade wars.

BANANA SPLIT

The banana has caused one of the biggest ever disputes between trade blocs. It lasted four years and involved a third of the WTO's countries. A group of fruit-selling companies in the US, backed by five South American banana-exporting nations, complained about tariffs that the EU used to support banana-growing countries in Africa and the Caribbean. The US said that the EU was favouring its former colonies at the expense of South American growers and US companies. The EU argued that it was supporting farmers in accordance with aid agreements it had signed in 1975.

Banana war settled?

The US retaliated by putting huge tariffs on EU imports into the US. This meant that many businesses in the EU that relied on trade with the US suffered. The WTO agreed with the US and said that the EU had broken a series of trade rules. The EU eventually adjusted its subsidy policy, but there are still people who

Although the 'banana war' is officially over, growers in former EU colonies are rapidly going out of business.

haven't recovered from the banana battle. Because the EU subsidies were designed to help banana growers in impoverished former colonies, without the money the growers are going out of business. One Jamaican newspaper recently reported that ministers from the Windward Islands were visiting Europe to make the EU understand that Caribbean banana producers were on the verge of disaster.

Recently, the US and EU had a steel 'trade war' because the US added tariffs to foreign imports to protect its own steel industry.

STEEL WAR

In 2002, the US government put tariffs on steel products imported into the country. Cheaper foreign imports were big competition for more expensive US steel, and by blocking imports the US government hoped to protect the US steel industry. When the EU and eight other steel-producing countries complained to the WTO, the US steel tariffs were found to be illegal.

The US wants to keep the subsidies on US cotton.

Retaliation

A WTO panel said the EU could retaliate if it wanted to by putting equal tariffs on US products imported into Europe.

While the EU was preparing a tariff list, the US government complained to the WTO about another issue. This time it was genetically modified (GM) crops, not steel. They accused Europe of acting illegally by discouraging GM food crops in Europe. Even though GM food may have serious environmental effects, the US wanted to put trade first. This new dispute made trade relations even worse between the EU and the US.

Tariffs dropped

The EU's retaliation would have meant that far fewer products would have been imported from the US into the EU. This would have led to job and business losses in the run-up to the 2004 US presidential election. So in December 2003, President Bush decided to drop the US steel tariffs to protect his presidency. This wasn't well received in the steel-producing states of Ohio, West Virginia and Pennsylvania. It is unlikely that trade could ever be fair to everyone.

CANCUN COTTON WAR SETTLED?

The Brazilian government complained about US cotton subsidies at the Cancun conference in 2003. By April 2004, they had won a landmark ruling. The WTO found that most subsidies given to US cotton farmers were illegal because they caused dumping.

A big step

Brazil's triumph was the first time a developing country has won such a major trade dispute at the WTO. It could represent the first of many rulings that reduce agricultural subsidies in the US and Europe. In June 2004, the US government said it would fight the WTO ruling, and was prepared to support the continued use of subsidies. The dispute over cotton

is set to continue. If the US does cut cotton subsidies, it will mean farmers in Brazil and west Africa will gain, but cotton farmers in the US will lose out.

GLOBAL CORPORATIONS

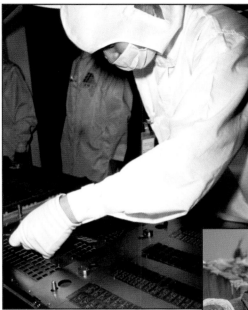

Foreign direct investments can improve the standard of living in a developing country. But withdrawing them can be devastating.

Global corporations are a powerful force in the global economy. Their size and number have changed the patterns of global trade and contributed to the growth in the international economy. The foreign direct investments – or FDI – that flow into a country when companies decide to set up new offices or factories can transform the standard of

living for people in a city or region. The benefits can also spread into healthcare facilities and education. But it can destroy livelihoods if the FDI is suddenly withdrawn.

SUPPLY CHAINS

Considering the size and influence of global corporations, the number of people directly employed is surprisingly few. Though making up 70 per cent of global trade, corporations directly employ between just 17 and 26 million people. There are, however, many more people indirectly employed by global corporations. Companies like IBM, Motorola, Nike or GAP 'sub-contract' business to factories which aren't owned or managed by them. Nike employs 20,000 people directly. Yet over 500,000 people around the world manufacture Nike products. In a supply chain that is large and complicated, human rights and environmental issues often appear.

But it is often the way in which a business chooses to conduct itself, rather than the size and the complexity of the business, that leads to environmental and human rights issues.

Who benefits?

When reports of environmental damage or human rights abuse emerge from a country, city or region where a global corporation has invested, people ask who is benefiting more: the company or the host country? The level of profits or the number of sales a company makes each year are easy to assess, but measuring the benefits – and the costs – to a country isn't always that simple.

Environmental costs

Prawn farmers in Indonesia have lost livelihoods because waste from an oil-refinery is pumped into the ocean where they fish. In southern India, local farmers protested when dangerous levels of a toxic chemical called cadmium were found in the waste produced by a soft drinks factory.

It is argued that the more relaxed environmental laws in poorer countries attract global corporations who would face tighter controls in their country of origin. Penalising companies who pollute the environment can make companies less irresponsible. Cases of irresponsible practices by corporations have led people to argue that developing countries have become 'eco-dumping' grounds for richer nations.

Have you ever thought about who made the clothes you wear?

Human cost

The costs to people's health reported in sweatshops in China or Bangladesh suggest that foreign direct investment (FDI) doesn't always improve people's standard of living. The real benefits of FDI are actually reduced by the cost of human rights abuses. When global corporations are blamed for these human rights abuses, they often argue that they're not the only ones responsible for the labour standards.

But who is responsible?

When reports of human rights abuse or environmental damage occur, it is difficult to know who to blame. Some argue that cultural differences and the local government are responsible for different attitudes to human rights and labour standards. Others say that large orders and last-minute deadlines to make products for foreign companies puts too much pressure on factory owners, employees and governments. If a corporation doesn't get its own way, there is always the worry that it will simply sub-contract the work and move production elsewhere.

Corporate responsibility

Levi Strauss – the jeans manufacturer – has a factory in the Dominican Republic in the Caribbean. The factory offers a day-care centre for its workers, has cheap transport laid on to and from work and provides education programmes.

Global corporations have a strong influence over how people are treated. In addition, businesses benefit from a healthy and educated workforce.

Mind the GAP?

The clothing company GAP was heavily targeted by the anti-globalisation protests. Bad media publicity led to people boycotting their products. This forced GAP to look at working standards in their factories. In 2003, GAP stopped doing business with over 50 factories around the world for not meeting with GAP's 'code of conduct'.

However, codes of conduct and social responsibility reports don't make it easier to monitor and manage long and complex supply chains. Some argue that companies like GAP shouldn't decide the working standards. They say it should be the people who work and run the country who do that.

A LIVING WAGE

More people could have a better standard of living if global companies encouraged factories to pay a 'living wage'. Paying a living wage means giving people enough to afford basic needs like food, accommodation, healthcare and education. We, as consumers, must also help. We need to learn to pay a realistic price for goods and services. That way, companies can increase wages instead of cutting costs.

Consumers are always on the look-out for the cheapest price. Consumers must pay a realistic price if workers are to improve their standard of living.

Free trade zones: Maquila story

Governments can also create free trade zones (FTZs) inside the borders of their own country. FTZs are scattered all over the world in places like Dubai, Costa Rica and Mauritius.

The Mexican government started an FTZ during the 1960s in a town called Ciudad Juárez in northern Mexico. The idea was to attract US companies by allowing them to import anything they needed without paying tax. In return, companies employed Mexicans and exported everything they made out of Mexico.

US companies flocked to take advantage of cheap labour, low rents and no tax. These US factories in Mexico are known as 'maquiladoras'. By 2000, there were 3,600 maquiladoras employing over one million people. The factories exported US $80 billion worth of electronic goods and car parts. This resulted in the Mexican economy gaining US $18 billion.

Critics of FTZs argue that workers are exploited and the environment damaged. They point to the Mexican town's drug addiction problems, poor housing, low wages for workers and pollution. They also argue that US companies benefit most, taking a bigger portion of profits than the community who makes the goods. Companies, not people or the Mexican government, are more powerful in Ciudad Juárez.

39

FAIRTRADE

There is a growing awareness of the problems and debates that surround global trade. This awareness has begun to affect the kinds of products that consumers buy in supermarkets and local shops. Because it's difficult for consumers to judge how fairly traded products are, FAIRTRADE labels and organisations across western Europe and North America try to make these judgements on behalf of consumers.

WHAT IS 'FAIRTRADE'?

FAIRTRADE is a way for producers and consumers to trade based on mutual benefit and respect. FAIRTRADE producers are found in poor areas of the world. By entering into a FAIRTRADE partnership, they are guaranteed to receive a fair price for their work. The price must cover their costs and give them a living wage. They get better access to markets in richer countries. Sustainable environmental practices and respect for people's rights are encouraged.

Labelling

There is a formal process for certifying food products that are produced under FAIRTRADE terms. In the UK, the Fairtrade Foundation's consumer label, the FAIRTRADE mark indicates whether a product meets strict FAIRTRADE standards. TransFair USA is the only independent certifier of FAIRTRADE products in the US.

The Fairtrade Foundation and TransFair USA along with 16 other national initiatives are members of the worldwide FAIRTRADE standard setting and certification organisation, Fairtrade Labelling Organisations International (FLO). FLO certifies more than one million growers in 60 countries. FLO inspectors visit farms and co-operatives to assess whether they've met FAIRTRADE criteria.

Global trade in food

Today there are over one million small-scale producers worldwide involved in FAIRTRADE, and sales in the US and Europe are growing fast. Mangoes from Burkina Faso and chocolate from Ghana are two of the FAIRTRADE food products sold in over 100,000 shops all over the world.

The UK FAIRTRADE mark (top) and the US FAIRTRADE logo (below) indicate official FAIRTRADE products.

FAIRTRADE

'Production for use, not for profit'

Towards the end of the 19th century, a 'Co-operative Movement' began in Europe. Groups like the Co-operative Wholesale Society in Britain re-invested the profits they made back into a network of 'co-op' members. These co-op members traded goods and services with one another.

By the 1960s, alternative trade was popular in the US and UK. In the early 1980s in the UK, organisations like Equal Exchange started selling coffee to support countries like Vietnam and Mozambique. In 1989, the Max Havelaar Foundation in the Netherlands launched the FAIRTRADE label. It encouraged the formation of other FAIRTRADE organisations, including The Fairtrade Foundation, The International Federation for Alternative Trade and the European Fair Trade Association.

In 1991, Oxfam, Traidcraft, Twin Trading and Equal Exchange started a company called Cafédirect. Today, Cafédirect is the UK's largest FAIRTRADE hot drinks company. Cafédirect also produce FAIRTRADE tea and chocolate and their actions have encouraged some supermarkets to produce their own FAIRTRADE drinks.

In the UK, an organisation called the Ethical Fashion Forum is taking steps to create a FAIRTRADE fashion label, similar to the one used for food products. This would tell consumers whether or not what they choose to wear is giving people a chance to benefit from fairer trade.

ETHICAL CONSUMERS

An ethical consumer buys a product for taste and price, like any other consumer. But they also want to know where and how a particular product has reached the shops. Most ethical consumers are prepared to pay a slightly higher price if it means communities benefit more and no unnecessary damage is done to the natural environment.

Unrealistic?

The FAIRTRADE movement has been criticised for not being realistic. Most people walking through a supermarket are more concerned with how much money they've got in their pocket or bank accounts. They'd rather save money so they can go on holiday or buy a new car. People, critics argue, don't buy products with their ethics. They often simply want to spend less money.

FAIRTRADE has transformed some coffee agriculture into a profitable occupation that farmers are able to do with dignity.

Niche market

Critics argue that the growth in FAIRTRADE will level out soon and show that it's nothing more than a 'niche market' within much bigger national and global economies. They suggest that it's only possible for an ethical niche market to grow in richer nations where people don't have to struggle daily to earn a living. The FAIRTRADE movement is just too small to make any real difference to the billion-plus people living in poverty.

More red tape

There are also doubts about how much the small-scale farmers and manufacturers actually benefit. FAIRTRADE does help communities that are involved in co-operative networks, but what about those people who are not involved?

As we have seen, to be part of a FAIRTRADE network, producers and suppliers have to meet certain standards. These standards help consumers judge what is fairly traded. But it's argued that these standards are just more regulations and rules: 'red tape' that makes economic growth slower and makes it more difficult for people in poorer nations to benefit from global trade.

The future

Despite the criticism that the FAIRTRADE movement has received, it does give producers control over their lives. FAIRTRADE brings financial certainty, allowing producers to plan their lives better, and make decisions about health and education for their children and about their products.

A FAIRTRADE story

Kuapa Kokoo means 'good cocoa farmers' in Twi, one of Ghana's languages. It's also been the name of a cocoa farming co-operative in Ghana's Ashanti region since 1993. Today, nearly 45,000 farmers are involved in Kuapa Kokoo.

In the early 1990s, trade liberalisation in Ghana allowed private companies licences to trade cocoa, and so Kuapa Kokoo was set up to allow growers to benefit more directly from exports.

Because FAIRTRADE companies in Europe and North America guarantee a fair price, farmers are benefiting from stable prices and earning a living wage. There is enough money in the co-operative to buy new farm equipment and build new wells.

In 1998, Kuapa Kokoo launched its own FAIRTRADE chocolate bar with a company called The Day Chocolate Company in the UK. Kuapa Kokoo's farmers own one-third of this company, share in its profits and contribute to how it is run.

FAIRTRADE

BETTER INVESTMENT

The increasing demand for FAIRTRADE practices means that many other global organisations are looking for more ethical ways to invest.

In 1976, the Grameen Bank in Bangladesh began lending small amounts of money to farmers who had no chance of getting loans from national banks. Today, Grameen lends to over two million people and has over 1,000 branches serving 40,000 villages. Known as 'microcredit', this way of lending money has encouraged more banks across the world to re-think how they invest in poorer nations.

Renewable energy

In 2000, the oil company Shell began investing in small businesses in Uganda that used renewable energy. Funding fruit farmers and honey growers who wanted to invest in solar power, Shell decided to invest over US $450 million in a longer-term project, rather than a one-off aid donation.

By making tourism more responsible and fairer, people in poorer countries benefit. Profits are re-invested in local schools and healthcare facilities.

43

BETTER THAN NOTHING?

The FAIRTRADE movement has increased people's awareness of different ways in which workers do not benefit from global trade. Although buying FAIRTRADE products is unlikely to reduce the gap between rich and poor countries overnight, this awareness means global corporations, governments and international organisations like the IMF and WTO are under more pressure to consider the problems of unfair trade. They are under pressure to cancel world debt, make decisions about trade rules more openly and to re-invest profits into communities. The power of ethical consumers is increasing, but governments and corporations still have a more direct impact on making sure that more people benefit from global trade.

CHRONOLOGY

4000 BC – Humans began moving along hilltops above river valleys that became known paths for travelling, herding animals, escaping or attacking enemies. These became the first trade routes.

3500 BC – The invention of wheeled vehicles in Mesopotamia encouraged trade of commodities like timber and grain over longer distances.

2900 BC – Egyptian boats began to explore the Indian Ocean. They traded slaves, ivory, gemstones and spices from the east African coast.

2500-1700 BC – People of the Indus civilisation traded along the banks of the Indus river valley, an area which covers modern-day Pakistan, northern India, Afghanistan, Tajikistan and south-west China.

312 BC-476 AD – The Roman Empire built a road system of over 80,000 km which made military conquest and effective running of the Empire possible. The road network across western Europe and northern Africa later provided highways for great migrations into the Empire and the movement of Christianity across western Europe.

150 BC-1500s AD – The Silk Road joined east Asia, the Middle East and Europe from ancient to medieval times. Spanning some 6,400 km, gold, silk and wool were the most valuable commodities carried along the route.

1492-1504 – Christopher Columbus, son of a weaver living in Genoa, Italy, began making voyages from Portugal across the Atlantic. On his first voyage he found himself in the Caribbean Islands. On the second voyage he founded 'Isabella', the first European city in the New World. On his third and final voyage he reached South America. This maritime achievement encouraged other European sailors and traders to explore the oceans of the world and marked the beginning of European colonialism.

1500-1800 – Vasco da Gama's explorations of western India, via sea routes around Africa at the Cape of Good Hope, encouraged more European traders to search for wealth overseas. As the voyagers travelled further, trade increased and so did the influence of European religion and political power across the globe. Organisations like the English East India Company controlled trade in spices, tea, coffee, tobacco and rubber for the financial benefit of the British Empire.

1765 – James Watt improved the design of the steam engine which led to Nicholas-Joseph Cugnot creating a steam carriage that travelled on roads in France, and Richard Trevithick to create the first steam locomotive to work on a railway in England in 1804.

1876 – Alexander Graham Bell was granted a patent for his invention of the telephone. The Bell Telephone Company created the American Telephone and Telegraph Company in 1885 to establish long-distance telephone communication. Today, the same company is more commonly known as AT&T.

1896 – Guglielmo Marconi invented a wireless means of communicating which led to the creation of long-distance radio.

1860-1945 – By the end of the 19th century, European colonialists turned to Africa in search of natural resources needed by the growing wealth and population in Europe following the industrial revolution. This led to areas of Africa being governed more directly by London, Lisbon and Paris.

1919 – Arthur Brown and John Alcock piloted the first aeroplane across the Atlantic. By the 1920s the first commercial airlines began to carry mail. The increased speed and range of these small aircraft made non-stop flights over the world's oceans and continents possible.

1944 – The Bretton Woods meeting took place in the US. Led by the US, the UK and the former Soviet Union, these nations discussed with 44 others, how best to create a stable and peaceful economy after the Second World War. They agreed to set up the IMF and the International Bank for Reconstruction and Development (which later became the World Bank). They also agreed to begin a series of 'rounds' to debate international trade laws.

1947 – The first international trade 'round' was held in Geneva involving 23 nations. It is called the General Agreements on Tariffs and Trade (GATT).

1970s – A sudden rise in oil prices led to an economic downturn in many developing countries which then began borrowing heavily from banks in western Europe. This is where the debt crisis for many nations started.

1983 – The internet was created. This revolutionised communication and banking in the late 20th century.

1989 – The first FAIRTRADE label was launched by the Max Havelaar Foundation in the Netherlands.

1995 – The World Trade Organisation headquarters was set up in Geneva after the final GATT rounds in Uruguay came to an end.

1991-1998 – What began as a time of growth for economies in south-east Asia turned into an economic crisis. This was the first time in history that a major economic depression had been caused by the free movement of investors' capital over national borders.

45

1999 – Anti-globalisation and anti-capitalist protests were held in Seattle, USA. This marked the beginning of several mass demonstrations. There were some violent clashes, but these demonstrations helped to spread an increasing awareness of how unfair trade can create poor working conditions and environmental problems and increase global inequality.

2004 – The charity Oxfam opened a coffee chain in the UK that sells only FAIRTRADE products. One of its coffee brands – Cafédirect – raised £5 million when shares for the company were sold on the London Stock Exchange. FAIRTRADE products are gaining a larger share of food sales in supermarkets and retailers in western Europe and North America. Other businesses are beginning to seek out the 'ethical consumer' – especially in clothes manufacturing and banking.

Organisations and Glossary

Cafédirect
City Cloisters
Suite B2, 196 Old Street
London EC1V 9FR
UK
Tel: +44 (0) 20 7490 9520
Email: info@cafedirect.co.uk
Website: www.cafedirect.co.uk
Cafédirect is the UK's largest *Fairtrade* hot drinks company.

Fairtrade Foundation
Room 204
16 Baldwin's Gardens
London EC1N 7RJ
UK
Tel: +44 (0) 20 7405 5942
Fax: +44 (0) 20 7405 5943
Email: mail@fairtrade.org.uk
Website: www.fairtrade.org.uk
Fairtrade Foundation is an organisation that publicises and reports on *Fairtrade* issues. It sells *Fairtrade* goods and sets *Fairtrade* standards.

Human Rights Watch
350 Fifth Avenue, 34th Floor
New York
NY 10118-3299
USA
Tel: +1 (212) 290 4700
Fax: +1 (212) 736 1300
Email: hrwnyc@hrw.org
Website: www.hrw.org
Human Rights Watch protects human rights worldwide. It also investigates and exposes human rights violations.

International Fair Trade Association
30 Murdock Road
Bicester OX26 4RF
UK
Tel: +44 (0) 1869 249819
Fax: +44 (0) 1869 246381
Email: info@ifat.org.uk
Website: www.ifat.org
A global network of over 160 *Fairtrade* organisations in more than 50 countries, which works to improve the livelihoods and well-being of disadvantaged people in developing countries and to change the unfair structures of international trade.

Kijijivision – Fair Trade Photography
Colin Hastings (Founder and Director)
Tel: +44 (0) 20 8209 1974
Email: colin@kijijivision.org
Website: www.kijijivision.co.uk
Kijijivision's goal is to help indigenous photographers win a fairer share of the global market for images of the southern hemisphere.

Médecins Sans Frontières
Postal Address
PO Box 847
Broadway
NSW 2007
Australia
Tel: +612 9552 4933
Fax: +612 9552 6539
Email: office@sydney.msf.org
Website: www.msf.org.au
Médecins Sans Frontières is the world's leading independent humanitarian organisation for medical aid. They help those living on the edge of human tolerance.

Oxfam International
Suite 20, 266 Banbury Road
Oxford OX2 7DL
UK
Tel: + 44 (0) 1865 31 39 39
Fax: + 44 (0) 1865 31 37 70
Email: information@oxfaminternational.org
Website: www.oxfam.org
Oxfam is a charity that campaigns on global issues and supports development projects worldwide. It also publishes reports on global issues.

The Day Chocolate Company
4 Gainsford Street
London SE1 2NE
UK
Tel: +44 (0) 20 7378 6550
Fax: +44 (0) 20 7378 1550
Email: info@divinechocolate.com
Websites: www.divinechocolate.com
and www.dubble.co.uk
The Day Chocolate Company produces Divine and Dubble *Fairtrade* chocolate to bring delicious *Fairtrade* chocolate into the hearts, and mouths, of every chocolate lover in the country.

Traidcraft
Kingsway
Gateshead
Tyne & Wear NE11 0NE
U K
Tel: +44 (0) 191 491 0591
Fax: +44 (0) 191 497 6562
Email: comms@traidcraft.co.uk
Website: www.traidcraft.org.uk
Traidcraft work at national and international level advocating changes in trade rules to make them work in the interests of the poor. They are committed to reducing poverty throughout the world.

TransFair USA
1611 Telegraph Avenue, Suite 900
Oakland
CA 94612
USA
Email: info@transfairusa.org
Website: www.transfairusa.org
TransFair USA is a non-profit organisation and is the only independent, third-party certifier of *Fairtrade* practices in the United States.

United Nations Conference on Trade and Development
(UNCTAD)
Palais des Nations
8-14 Avenue de la Paix 1211
Geneva 10
Switzerland
Tel: +41 22 917 5809
Fax: +41 22 907 0043
Email: info@unctad.org
Website: www.unctad.org
United Nations body that discusses trade and development issues.

World Trade Organisation
(WTO)
Centre William Rappard
Rue de Lausanne 154
CH-1211 Geneva 21
Switzerland
Tel: +41 22 739 5111
Fax: +41 22 731 4206
Email: enquiries@wto.org
Website: www.wto.org

ORGANISATIONS AND GLOSSARY

Activists – Individuals or groups that challenge governments, political ideas or human rights abuse.

Biotechnology – The use of technology in biology.

Carbon dioxide – An atmospheric gas created when we breathe and when fossil fuels are burned.

Cartel – A group of people or organisations that agree to control the supply of a product.

Cash crop – A crop like coffee or cocoa that is grown for selling, not for personal consumption.

Civil war – A conflict between different groups within a country.

Debt – Money owed to another individual, organisation or country.

Developing countries – Countries in the process of becoming industrialised.

Embargo – Steps taken by organisations or governments to ban the import or export of certain goods for political or human rights reasons.

European Union (EU) – An economic and political alliance of 25 European countries.

Exploitation – The abuse of human rights.

Fossil fuels – Mined materials like oil or coal which come from the Earth.

Genetically modified (GM) – Naturally grown crops that have been altered using technology to improve crop yields or resistance to pests.

Human rights – The basic freedoms to which all humans are entitled – life, liberty, thought, expression and equality.

Investors – Individuals or companies who put money into other businesses or markets with hope or expectation of future financial benefits for themselves.

Labour – Employees or workers of a company or organisation.

Liberalisation – A series of government steps with the aim of relying on private business and free trade to increase economic growth.

Manufactured – A product that is made.

Market – A place where goods and services are sold.

Militia – A non-government military group.

Patent – An official record for a product or service that records an invention or ownership.

Pesticide – A chemical product used against pests that feed on crops.

Recession – Economic depression signalled by high unemployment.

Stock exchange or stock market – The place where company stocks and shares are bought and sold every day.

Stocks and shares – Companies sell 'shares' or 'stock' to raise money which they can invest back into their businesses. When somebody buys a share of a particular company, it literally means they are buying a part-ownership in it. The more shares you have in a company, the more of it you own.

Surplus – The over-production of a product.

Sweatshops – The term used to describe poor working conditions, mostly in manufacturing.

Trade unions – Organisations that support the rights of workers or employees.

Trafficking – The movement of people or goods. Human trafficking often involves transporting people away from their homes, by the threat or use of violence, deception, or coercion, so they can be exploited as forced or enslaved workers for sex or labour.

Viagra – Medicine used to treat sexual difficulties in men and sometimes women.

47

INDEX

Photo Credits:
Abbreviations: l-left, r-right, b-bottom, t-top, c-centre, m-middle
Front cover t, b & mc, back cover t, 1mc, 4bl, 6bl, 7br, 15tr, 21c, 26bl, 27bm, 28br, 32ml, 35 both, 37tl, 38mt, 40tr, 44tr, 45tr — Flat Earth. Front cover ml, 1ml, 3tr, 4tr, 12ct, 13b, 14bl, 17c, 17br, 18bl, 19bm, 20br, 24br, 25tr, 29br, 30ml, 34b, 37c, 39tl, 43t, 45bl — Corel. Front cover mr, 1mr — Jonas Jordan/Courtesy of the U.S Army. 2bl, 9tr, 10mr, 40bm, 41bm, 42br — Transfair USA. 2-3b, 5mt, 7ml, 8bl, 11br, 12mlt, 13tr, 14tr, 16tr all, 17tl, 21tl, 22 both, 23tr, 31c, 33 all, 38mr — Corbis. 5mr — Sony Ericsson. 6tr — Peter Manzelli/USDA. 8tl, 18br, 19tr, 25ml, 31t, 39ml, 42mt — Photodisc. 9br, 44bl — Ken Hammond/USDA. 11tl, 28tl, 39br — Select Pictures. 12mrt — Bill Tarpenning/USDA. 12mlb, 12mrb, 12bl, 12cb, 12br — Stockbyte. 15ml, 36tr — John Deere. 16br — Ingram Publishing. 19c — PFC Joshua Hutcheson/Courtesy of the U.S Army. 20t — SPC Jason Heisch/Courtesy of the U.S Army. 21br — NIH. 23tl — Médicins Sans Frontières. 23br — Tommy Gilligan/U.S. Navy. 24tr — Robin Ressler/USCG. 29tr — James Tourtellotte/U.S. Customs & Border Protection. 30br — Dorothea Lange/USDA. 36br — European Parliament. 40cl — Fairtrade Foundation.